D0901541

DEAD MEN RISING!

BUILDING GOD'S CHAMPIONS DURING PERILOUS TIMES!

CHUCK BREWSTER

DEAD MEN RISING!

Copyright ©2006

Chuck Brewster

Champions of Honor
P. O. Box 820
Gulf Breeze, FL 32562

ISBN Number: 0-9768775-6-2

All rights reserved under International Copyright law. This publication may not be reproduced, stored in a retrieval system, or transmitted in whole or in part, in any form or by any means, electronic, mechanical, photocopying, recording or otherwise, without prior express written permission of the Publisher.

All scripture references are taken from the New International Version of the Bible, unless otherwise noted.
The Holy Bible, New International Version
Copyright ©1978 by New York International Bible Society

Printed in the United States of America.

FOREWORD

A champion trains to become a champion and a coach is a champion of champions, helping them reach their goals. Coaches train champions to multiply themselves. Chuck is a multiplier, a Champion of Champions, and a visionary that sets a path for men to pursue God as passionate athletes might fight for crossing the goal line.

Promise Keepers brought men into the stadiums and recruited them for God. And when they left and asked "Now what?" God had Chuck perfectly positioned with answers to that question.

Having been a Secret Service Agent determined to save lives, God shifted his focus to eternal salvation. What better way to challenge men than to ask them --- "Die to yourselves and serve God and your fellow man!"

I support Chuck in his quest to bring men from "stadium events" into a lifelong quest of serving God every day in every area of their life. In today's world, we need to challenge our men with spiritual growth in worship, discipleship, and evangelism. That is Chuck's heart.

Coach Bill McCartney
Founder of Promise Keepers

DEDICATION

I want to dedicate this book to my wonderful wife, Rhonda, and our children, Chad and Lanie. Their encouragement gave me the focus, ability and wisdom to press through with God.

I would also like to thank Randy Jumper and Andrew Templeton whose editing and writing skills challenged me to continue hearing from God.

It would also be wrong not to mention the leaders of the men's movement like Ed Cole, Bill McCartney, and many others that impacted my life. The pastors I have had in the last 20 years also made a huge impression upon me to press into to God and let Him lead me in my ministry.

Finally, I want to thank Bob Armstrong for his assistance in completing this book. He is a Champion in the men's movement.

TABLE OF CONTENTS

RESURRECTING GOD'S CHAMPIONS

My desire in this book is that you will receive a new breath of God's Spirit in your life, your family, your relationship with God, and your particular situation. "Dead Men Rising" is not just about the dry bones in Ezekiel, or about resurrecting a men's movement, it is about you.

In the story of Ezekiel's vision of a "Valley of Dry Bones" found in chapter 37 verses 1-10, the Bible says,

"*The hand of the LORD was upon me, and He brought me out by the Spirit of the LORD and set me down in the middle of the valley; and it was full of bones. And He caused me to pass among them round about, and behold, there were very many on the surface of the valley; and lo, they were very dry. And He said to me, 'Son of man, can these bones live?' And I answered, 'O Lord GOD, Thou knowest.' Again He said to me, 'Prophesy over these bones, and say to them, "O dry bones, hear the word of the LORD." 'Thus says the Lord GOD to these bones, "Behold, I will cause breath to enter you that you may come to life. And I will put sinews on you, make flesh grow back on you, cover you with skin, and put breath in you that you may come alive; and you will know that I am the LORD."'*

"*So I prophesied as I was commanded; and as I prophesied, there was a noise, and behold, a rattling; and the bones came together, bone to its bone. And I looked, and behold, sinews were on them, and flesh grew, and skin covered them; but there was no breath in them. Then He said to me, 'Prophesy to the breath, prophesy, son of man, and say to the breath, "Thus says the Lord GOD, 'Come from the four winds, O breath, and breathe on these slain, that they come to life.'" So I prophesied as He commanded me, and the breath came into them, and they came to life, and stood on their feet, an exceedingly great army." – Ezekiel 37:1-10 (NASV)*

I want to reflect upon the state of men and the passive spirit of men within the United States today. I honestly believe that the state of men is very much like the valley of dry bones. We have rested in the valley and have become very dry because we have not been mentored, connected, nor filled and re-filled with the Holy Spirit. The Spirit gives us life, flesh, skin and moisture in our body, blessed to breathe and speak life into others. There are dry bones in the valley and God says to Ezekiel, "Speak and prophecy unto these bones."

There have been a lot of men coming into the men's movement that have risen up and said, "Spirit, breathe on me! Let's rise up and come alive!" There have been a lot of movements in the last one hundred years to try to get men to really come alive with God. They got one part of it, saying, "Okay, bones get up in the stadium." But when they left the stadium they were still a bunch of bones. They didn't have flesh. Some could not retain the new breath of life.

We need to continue prophesying the Word of God to men and the state of men in America today, in speaking to the bones.

We need to say to the men of America that are complacent in their walk with God or having no walk with God at all, "Get some flesh on your bones. Get into the Word of God and start putting meat on yourself. Start giving yourself some strength. Get some muscle on yourself. Get some sinew on you to hold your muscles together. Then seal it with your salvation that would be the skin holding the body together, skin that gives you identity in God. And, take care of your skin surrounding your body, or person, so that it is whole, in tact, and holy within." I believe that the breath is the very breath of the Holy Spirit that gives the body life and power.

Even as men came alive in the men's movement and started growing in the Word (meat) they continued to view doing things as an outlet for their expression of love of God. It became routine or a bodily function without the breath of life in the man himself, but a mere expression. The Word says, *"And I looked and behold sinews were on them and the flesh grew and skin covered them, but there was no breath in them."*

Today, in America, we need to breathe. We must have breath blown into us by the Holy Spirit.

Then God said, "Prophesy unto the breath. Prophesy son of man and say to the breath, 'Thus saith the Lord God.' Come from the four winds, the north, the south, the east, and the west, from every direction. Come from the four winds of breath, and breathe on these slain that they come to life." (verse 9)

You can have flesh. You can have skin. You can have bones that get up and walk from the grave, but unless you have life in you, you are really not going to be very productive as an army of God. You'll just be the walking dead.

God wants YOU to be a part of His army. You may not feel qualified, but He can begin to breathe a new breath of the Spirit within you. He can qualify you for His army, no matter what your circumstances or background. God literally covets a relationship with you.

There is a saying that goes like this, "It does more good to talk to God about men, than to talk to men about God." That speaks to the breath. The breath comes from God. We need to speak to God about the breath that needs to be breathed into the men that we are interacting with in our workplace, in our community, in our church, and in our own small, fellowship groups. We need to speak to God about the breath, and ask Him to send the breath of the Holy Spirit to make them come alive.

Why do we go through resources in Champions of Honor to develop our Biblical masculinity? So we can receive not only the flesh, the sinew and the skin, but allow the breath of God to come alive within us.

When that breath comes in, you come to life. As the word says in Ezekiel, then they stood to their feet as a vast army. The same can happen to you, right now, in your life.

Dead men are beginning to come out of their "grave clothes" of mediocrity and passivity in church.

As I look back at my time in the U.S. Secret Service while serving in the White House, I remember one of the first acts President Carter did after his inauguration was to order the military in the Washington District, not to wear their uniform while on duty. The administration did not want to see military uniforms. This was an apparent backlash from the Nixon days and an apparent need, felt by the President, to remove the military look of Washington, D.C. The Carter administration didn't want Washington to appear as a "military state."

President Carter was a graduate of Annapolis, a military man, yet he was the one taking our men and women out of uniform in the "Beltway" of Washington D.C. The President literally took the identity from them.

The military, during his administration, were "dead men." They were not allowed to be up on their feet as a vast army, but they were told to hide their identity and be passive, much like the men of the church today. We are told to behave and be "really nice guys" as John Eldridge writes.

I remember thinking, why would he do this, but as a good soldier, we don't question, we just do. I spent four years traveling with Jimmy Carter, and also growing in Christ, little-by-little. I went to church with President Carter and he would teach Sunday School. I would go in and stand in the back. Basically, I was guarding him. But I was also receiving "flesh" on my bones, because I was a fairly new Christian and needed to be developed so I would listen to the Word of God that he was teaching.

I am not saying that President Carter was a bad man. No, he was a good man. He was, and still is, a Christian man. My personal and political beliefs are just more conservative than his beliefs. But he had some positives. He had compassion. But some of his compassion was misplaced and misdirected in my opinion and weakened the country. He had the bones, the tendons, the flesh, but the Spirit sometimes would be lacking. He was very confident in himself.

I also reflect back to when Ronald Reagan was inaugurated as President. I was detailed out to California to assist in the transition of the Reagan Presidency from California to the White House. One of the first things I remember President Ronald Reagan did was to orchestrate the release of our hostages from Iran. Then he put the uniforms back on our military in our nation's capital. I thought then, "He is breathing into our nation patriotism once again."

President Reagan came in and brought a different breath. As he got that vast army and breathed life of affirmation into them, in essence, he said, "Put on your uniforms. Stand with your swords and your rifles. Be a vast army." Then the breath of life was breathed once again into our military and into our nation. The military had their identity. The nation stood proud as our nation impacted the world. When the President put our men and women back in uniform, they had identity and the breath of life once again went into those dry bones. As that life came back, we were able to accomplish much.

In 1987 I served as a Secret Service supervisor with Vice President George Bush. He became President in 1988 and I saw dignity and honor continue in our country. As we went to war in the Gulf, the honor of a risen army was evident. Even his "1,000 Points of Light" showed us how we could be our brother's keeper.

As I write this book, I am trying to give you some history of what I saw with my own eyes, standing backstairs at the White House, standing in front of the podiums where Presidents and Vice-Presidents spoke, standing outside meeting rooms where leaders of our world met and talked.

I do remember President Jimmy Carter as a great man by bringing Christian, Muslin, and Jew together when he hosted the Camp David Summit with President Sadat of Egypt and Prime Minister Begin of Israel. He was focused upon bringing a Middle East Peace Accord. Still, to this day, we are trying to bring about that peace. But if you would just go to the Word of God you would understand that peace will never, really truly come until the return of our Lord Jesus Christ.

In 1992, President Bill Clinton was elected. The first thing that he did when he came into his office was to create the "Don't Ask, Don't Tell" policy in our military. He took the air of the breath out of our military. But he had showed his positions before he got elected. He was even on a television talk show explaining his adulterous behavior prior to us electing him as President of the United States.

People ask me, "How could we ever elect someone like that?"

Remember this, we wouldn't allow Gary Hart to be elected as President because he had a woman sitting on his lap. But between the time Gary Hart ran for President and Bill Clinton ran for President, there was a change in the moral climate of the United States of America. We didn't elect a Bill Clinton until we became like Bill Clinton…an adulterous nation.

Speaking into the lives of the military then with a "Don't Ask, Don't Tell" policy was really not speaking life, it was speaking death. There is a difference in speaking life and speaking death. We have to understand, as we are building an Army of God, and as we are talking to God about men, we need to talk to God about sending the breath of the Holy Spirit to fill us. The Holy Spirit can give us a good life and a <u>Godly</u> life.

My reflections of my Secret Service and White House days impact my messages as I travel and speak in ministry. I try to bring my past experiences into application of what my life has been. I can't speak about your life, because I have not lived your life. I have only lived my life. I know that God brought me out of the government, much like Nehemiah. He supernaturally brought me into His house to help lead an army, connect men together, put flesh on bones that are dry; and to breathe life into men that are breathless.

The purpose of this book, "Dead Men Rising," is to help bring a new breath of life into the men's movement and to resurrect God's Champions.

Resurrecting God's Champions is not saying that we did not have champions before. We have had incidences of champions and you hear about them as the heroes of the faith; as the martyrs that have gone before us.

But God really wants an Army of God of Champions that will stand up and come together from the north, south, east and west, from all four winds, standing up ready to serve Him, a consecrated Army of Champions.

God really loves men. I am not saying that He loves them more than women. God loves the fellowship with men. He loves men who like to "buck up" to each other. He likes men that really are men. I know God loves all men, but my picture of God is that He does not desire a weak man. He wants a strong man. The Word of God keeps telling us how to be a strong man of God. God wants fellowship once again with men. He doesn't want just an acquaintance or a part-time relationship. He wants fellowship with us. He is calling together men's leaders all over the nation and the world to raise a vast army.

I believe the Word of God is a living word. It applies today as it did yesterday. History is also part of prophecy. I believe Ezekiel is speaking to the men of the world today to rise up as a vast army. I believe that through the efforts of Promise Keepers, Champions of Honor, Men of Integrity, Christian Men's Network, HonorBound, Mighty Men of Valor, and many other different men's organizations, we are putting breath into dry bones after flesh has been wrapped on them and skin has sealed them. We just need the vision and the message to get out with passion.

God is building an army for that last war. I believe right now, President George W. Bush, the leader of our nation, is giving a signal to the world in many ways such as going to a state approved and sanctioned, house church in China. Just by the President going, he showed the leaders and people of China that, "I am a Christian and I am going to one of your churches to worship God" … God is breathing life into the Chinese church.

God ordains and anoints every king, president, prime minister, and leader. No one gets authority except from God. No one can have authority over a nation unless God approves. That is hard to understand. But it is the Word, because every thing is subject to God.

Over the years, we have been sold a pack of lies. In the seventies, many feminists and sociologists said that men were "male chauvinistic pigs." We oppressed the feminist society, where they have a "glass ceiling." They couldn't get a high-paying job. In practical terms, it was true, because jobs and companies did have a glass ceiling. Women were not executive officers.

Many women have grown through that. But at the sake of the "slain", and many men were the slain, chopped up, mutilated, and thrown into that valley of dry bones by the feminist movement.

Men are necessary and we are not defined by women, but by God. The feminist movements of the seventies and eighties are starting to realize how much it takes keeping up with men. Men are work-wired, where women are relationship-wired. But now some women are toning back and saying, "Hey, motherhood isn't bad. I want to stay with my children and develop them." Women are coming back to how God wired them. It does not mean that women cannot be great entrepreneurs and leaders, but they are realizing men are not their enemy.

Anyone that uses religion to hold a woman down is wrong. God did not intend for religion to keep women in "their place." God wants women to be all that He made them to be.

In the Book of Genesis, God holds man accountable for the woman. We need to learn how to be Godly men, especially in relationship with women.

When you look in the Old Testament you will see that not everybody was honorable to God. At God's own house, they defiled the temples. They raped and they murdered. I don't mean just conquered and killed. I am talking about doing things that were despicable in the eyes of the Lord. They worshipped other gods. We are not different today than the church of old. We are just in a different place. But there came along, every so often, a vast army, that remnant of dry bones that rose up and brought it all together.

One of those commanders of that remnant who brought it all together was Nehemiah, a bodyguard for the king.

I want this book to change the way men think!

At the end of every chapter, I will ask questions that will provoke and challenge you to rise up as "Dead Men Rising."

1. Do you feel that God's breath is being breathed on men today?
2. What is it going to take to organize that army into an effective force for today?

BODYGUARDS...
Living for the Cause

A part of breathing new life into dry bones is the ability and desire to live for an honorable cause. It reminds me of the days that I served as bodyguard to presidents. As a bodyguard for the leader of a nation, one can be consumed with the importance of one's position. One has the power of life and death over someone and influence with the leader one protects. An effective bodyguard must die to self and put the leader's life first. This is not a natural act, but a learned or conditioned response after much training and dedication to duty.

Imagine yourself with this responsibility – the safety of a world leader. The influence and importance you have is pivotal. Imagine the sense of fulfillment you have in knowing that you are playing an important role in the world's affairs because you protect this leader. But now imagine you also having great compassion for your people. You see your homeland and are dismayed by the spiritual decline that brings a downward spiral of trouble and disgrace to your nation?

What can you do? What can any one man do? For all your "important" responsibilities, you watch as that which you love most, slips into moral decay. You know that God uses people to accomplish His perfect plan. You know He is looking for that man who has the compassion and the willingness to lead His people back to being "One Nation

Under God." You know you are that man—that champion who is part of God's Army – the man to "rebuild the walls of Jerusalem."

Nehemiah knew he was that man. As "Cupbearer to the King" it was his responsibility to protect and serve the most powerful leader in the world. Distraught with the knowledge that his people were in <u>trouble</u> and <u>disgraced</u> because of the deteriorated condition of the walls of Jerusalem, Nehemiah felt the call from God to do something for his people.

As a former modern-day "cupbearer to the King," I understand some of what Nehemiah went through. In some ways, my story parallels Nehemiah's story. My walls that need re-built are the walls of the family. I only hope to be able to help rebuild the families of America with the same effectiveness as he rebuilt the walls of Jerusalem.

Having served my nation as a Secret Service Agent for 23 years, guarding numerous political candidates and public officials, including Presidents of the United States, I identify with Nehemiah. I retired from the Secret Service in 1998, when God called me into ministry full-time.

Just like Nehemiah, I was driven by the need of my nation and a vision for what God could do through me. I saw the need of our country through my travels in the Secret Service. God prepared me for a mission by allowing me to see the condition of our land long before I knew my calling. My travels left me heart-broken. I was dismayed at the condition of families in America.

Nehemiah had a physical wall of protection to rebuild, but for me, the breach in America is the breakdown of the family. The father vacuum and the lack of godly male leadership is so widespread. I am convinced it is the root cause of most of the social and spiritual ills of America. In fact, the statistics of the Heritage Foundation were recently quoted by Cal Thomas, saying, "The root cause for poverty and crime in America is the lack of fathers in the family."

My move, like Nehemiah's, is a miracle in itself. During a time of intense prayer, God gave a vision to me of a great harvest of men waiting to be reaped.

In 1990, following a typical "burnt pancake breakfast" at my church, I drove my car around some land in Gaithersburg, Maryland. I was praying for God's blessing for our church to purchase a piece of land. I was tired of meeting in a school and wanted a more permanent location.

While I was driving around the 50 acres, the Holy Spirit came over me in such a powerful way that I had to pull my car over to the side of the road. In the middle of my prayer, I realized I had pulled over next to a large cornfield.

During that prayer, God gave me a vision of millions of men with their hands stretched to heaven. That cornfield turned into rows of men lifting up holy hands toward God without anger or dispute (I Timothy 2:8). God spoke to me that I should "Raise an Army" of men and train them to be ready for His service. I had no idea yet what it meant and wondered how I could do such a thing.

Over the next seven years, my passion to reach men grew. I became involved in my local church and witnessing inside the Secret Service. During the Promise Keepers event, "Stand in the Gap", where over 1.4 million men gathered for prayer in Washington, God again began to speak to me. On that day, I saw the vision birthed within me seven years earlier begin to unfold. I looked up and saw nearly two million hands lifted to God just like that day in the cornfield. I thought my vision had been fulfilled. I cried out to God to help me understand what was happening. Was my vision complete? I didn't really think so.

Then I felt the Holy Spirit saying to me that the vision was just beginning. Something in my life was about to change.

Within one year, I was asked to lead a national ministry to men of a large denomination. At the time I was only vaguely familiar with the ministry God was calling me to lead. Like Nehemiah, I saw the need around me and I cried out to God to heal our land. Like Nehemiah, God chose me to be an instrument of that healing.

My road from the White House to God's House was unique, but not too different from what God wants to do with every man. God is calling each of us to lay down our lives for the vision He has called us to fulfill. Every man in America needs to lay down all he is, in order that God may then begin to truly use him in His Army.

The change within me happened when God told me to lay it down and follow Him.

On the road to God's House, I stopped off at the White House as God prepared me to lead men in America. With all of my Secret Service assignments around the nation, God used me in different churches to see first hand, from the pew, the needs of ordinary men. Seeing the duality of how our nation and how God's Kingdom works, has made me unique in understanding the men of this nation. Raising an Army of prepared men is what God wants and

I am determined to deliver.

God has instructed me to help breathe life into men that are breathless.

1. Are you spiritually preparing to lay down your life for God's cause?
2. What are you doing to help stop the lack of fathers in American families?

CHAPTER 2

TRAINING...
Men for Significance

"Shots fired!"

Secret Service agents train their whole career to react to those words, hoping they never hear them. As President Ronald Reagan exited the Washington Hilton on March 30, 1981, those words filled my earpiece. Instantly, my fellow agents and I put into action plans and training we had learned. No one had time to think what to do; our training took over. I headed for George Washington Hospital to secure the area; others went to the White House. Each of us instinctively reacted with precision and speed because we had trained for this moment all of our careers.

My friend Tim McCarthy's training kicked in quicker than the rest of us. As the President left the Hilton and approached his limo, John Hinckley pulled a small handgun and fired several shots at the President. At the sound of the first shot, Agent McCarthy placed himself between Hinckley and the President forming a human shield. The second shot struck him in the stomach rather than hitting the President. His split second decision saved the life of President Ronald Reagan. Tim McCarthy became a hero, because he, an ordinary man, performed his job in an extraordinary way. Yet his actions were the result of years of training, training that enabled him to make a split-second response.

What are you trained to do? When a difficult situation

comes, how will you respond?

Will you be forced to pause and think through the issue or will you be prepared to make the right decision in enough time to make the most impact?

As a champion in the making, God will cause flesh to be put on your dry bones. But it is a process. It doesn't happen overnight. As you receive more training, you will receive more flesh.

I am convinced that the greatest challenge the church faces today is training men to become the kind of leaders in their families and churches God intended them to be. I have traveled and spoken with hundreds of men who are longing for this kind of training. It is necessary for pastors and men's leaders to take the lead in training men in the ways of godly masculinity. The enemy is attacking the family and the church like never before. We need men to stand in the gap and protect them. When church leaders do not train men to act according to the Word of God, their men's actions will resemble those of the world.

The Bible says in 1 Corinthians 9:25–27 (NIV):

Everyone who competes in the games goes into strict training. They do it to get a crown that will not last; but we do it to get a crown that will last forever. Therefore I do not run like a man running aimlessly; I do not fight like a man beating the air. No, I beat my body and make it my slave so that after I have preached to others, I myself will not be disqualified for the prize.

God is calling men to train in such a way as to win the prize. Some men feel they are trained because they attend Sunday School and are faithful to church. Sunday School is important and necessary, but developing prepared men involves much more. It involves a daily regimen of repetitive training, coupled with the breath of the Holy Spirit.

When we don't submit to daily conditioning, we look like the prizefighter who is punching the air. His form and technique may look good, but it is ineffective in connecting, engaging, and defeating the enemy. That is no way to finish the race. It takes a strong, well-trained man – a man full of the power of the Holy Spirit – to stand in the gap for his family, church, and community.

Men cannot stand in the gap under their own power.

"How do I do it? Where do I begin?" seems to be the question on the hearts and minds of most leaders and champions when it comes to training men. This is a very important question because I believe not only do you get what you pay for – you also get what you train for.

First, **TRAIN MEN IN GOD'S WORD**. Men can't be trained using worldly tools. There is no substitute for God's Word when training men to be spiritual leaders. The Bible says in Psalm 11:3, *"When the foundations are being destroyed, what can the righteous do?"* This verse addresses the problem in society and the church – the wearing away of a godly foundation in society and its effect on the men in the church. The erosion of the moral foundation of America has impacted the family and consequently the church and its ministries. Biblical illiteracy in our churches is at epidemic proportions. Psalms 119:11 also says, *"I have hidden your word in my heart that I might not sin against you." (NIV)*

There is no substitute for biblical teaching. You need to study and memorize the Word of God. Many men's programs are "topical, feel-good" discussions but do not take men into the Word of God. Men who are grounded in the Word are men who are properly trained. They are the ones receiving that skin on their dry bones.

Secondly, **LEAD MEN INTO A PASSIONATE RELATIONSHIP WITH GOD**. Transforming men in a society that does not believe in absolute moral truth is difficult. The only way to rebuild a moral foundation is to capture men's hearts and lead them in a passionate pursuit of God. Men want to give their lives to something and be challenged. We must present a passionate faith to men and then challenge them to live it.

God gave me a unique perspective in transforming men. The Secret Service is responsible for the total security of the protectee. When danger appears, agents "cover and evacuate" the person they protect. "Cover and evacuate" means exactly that – cover the protectee with your own body and evacuate him/her to safety. This scenario is practiced hundreds of times and every possible situation is trained for repeatedly. Due to this exhaustive training, agents are able to overcome the natural human tendency of self-survival, thinking only of the mission. That is passion. Transitioning from a "dead man" to a "live wire" requires that same passion.

It takes passionate men to devote all of their attention to their mission. You can be passionate about many things, but for how many of your passions will you die? Perhaps you would die for family, country, or cause, so why not die to your selfish desires and come alive with a godly purpose? Transformed men are no longer satisfied with just *doing* church. They want to *be* the church. They become passionate men—warriors for God.

Third, **CHURCH LEADERS MUST TAKE AN ACTIVE ROLE IN LEADING MEN'S MINISTRY.** The senior pastor must be the head trainer, and he must build relationships with his men. Men who are trained and who have godly relationships with other men will reach men for Christ. But training and relationships have been difficult for men to accomplish because men's ministry has typically been focused on what we *do* as men, not who we *are*. Sitting on a pew and listening to a Sunday message is not training; it takes more than a Sunday sermon to develop a passionate man of God. Leaders must lead their men in a closer walk with God. Passion can't be produced; it has to be reproduced. Passion is caught, not taught.

All Secret Service agents go through training, even supervisors. In fact, supervisors lead the sessions. They know they share common tactical goals with their trainees and need to be transparent with them to operate in unity. Training is done as a team, so results are as a team. Discipline and training can be boring, but often lifesaving. Routine training can develop a complacency that results in inattentive behavior, but repetitive training develops conditioning. Purpose and passion must characterize Secret Service training so agents are positioned for sacrifice.

When men come alive in relationship with Jesus Christ and their pastor, they are dynamically transformed. As men partner with their pastor, they build walls of protection against the enemy through prayer and watchfulness. Men must guard against the devil's desire to thwart the process of spiritual transformation in their lives. Jesus said in Matthew 26:41, "*Watch and pray so that you will not fall into temptation. The spirit is willing, but the body is weak."*

As a men's ministry champion in the making, men must operate differently from the world. You must be trained when the enemy shows up and prepared to accomplish the mission. Many pastors I have talked with say time is the major reason they can't do more with their men. The bottom line is men need training, and the pastor is the one who must lead the way. It is imperative that pastors find time in their schedules to disciple and train their men.

Agent McCarthy would not have accomplished his mission without preparation. At times you may feel the task of being a champion is too burdensome, but resist this tendency and continue to challenge men to fulfill God's plan for their lives. God wants your best. You can start rebuilding the crumbling foundation of our culture by investing your life in men and joining them in a passionate pursuit of God. The church of Jesus Christ needs men of significance who have a passion to serve and who are positioned to make a difference in their world, with the breath of life breathed into them by the Holy Spirit.

Do you know a bunch of sold out men, standing firm in their faith and walking it out in their families, community and church? Or do you know "spectators" and/or weekend warriors attending burnt pancake breakfasts?

Transforming men today in a crumbling society where the majority of men do not believe in absolute moral truth is a challenge to every pastor in America. The only way to rebuild this foundation is to capture men's hearts and lead them in a passionate pursuit of God. Rebuilding male leadership back into the church takes strong and courageous men who realize who they are in Christ, standing firm while reproducing themselves in that knowledge. No more dead men's bones, but a resurrected champion for God.

Traditional men's ministry will not do the job. It has become a pancake breakfast men's club, not a gathering of *passionate*, *prepared*, and *positioned* men forming a vast army of God. The answer is training and relationships! Men trained and in godly relationships with other men will reach men for Christ. But, training and relationships are hard for men to accomplish since men's ministry has been what we **do** as men, not who we **are.**

The Bible tells us we are to stand firm with Jesus? It says we are to be a <u>*willing sacrifice*</u>, transformed by the

Renewing of our mind.

"*Therefore, I urge you, brothers, in view of God's mercy, to offer your bodies as living sacrifices, holy and pleasing to God-this is your spiritual act of worship. Do not conform any longer to the pattern of this world, but be transformed by the renewing of your mind. Then you will be able to test and approve what God's will is-his good, pleasing and perfect will.*" (Romans 12:1-2)

Trained to win.

"*Everyone who competes in the games goes into strict training. They do it to get a crown that will not last; but we do it to get a crown that will last forever. Therefore I do not run like a man running aimlessly; I do not fight like a man beating the air. No, I beat my body and make it my slave so that after I have preached to others, I myself will not be disqualified for the prize.*" (1 Corinthians 9:25-27)

Deployed in power.

"*Therefore go and make disciples of all nations, baptizing them in the name of the Father and of the Son and of the Holy Spirit, and teaching them to obey everything I have commanded you. And surely I am with you always, to the very end of the age.*" (Matthew 28:19-20)

"*But you will receive power when the Holy Spirit comes on you; and you will be my witnesses in Jerusalem, and in all Judea and Samaria, and to the ends of the earth.*" (Acts 1:8 NIV)

That means we need to <u>reproduce</u> men who are:

1. Passionate – Willing to sacrifice their life for others.

2. Prepared – Trained to overcome natural tendencies of the world.

3. Positioned – Deployed into their unique world of influence.

1. What are you trained to do?
2. Are you prepared to make the right decision when times get tough?
3. When difficulties come, how will you respond?
4. How much training do you have from God's Word?
5. Are you passionate enough in your personal relationship with God?

CHAPTER 3

CHANGE...
A Necessary Focus.

I stand in awe of what God is doing in men today. No longer is there a "sea of dry bones," but the Holy Spirit is rising up true, godly champions. In order to be ready for the return of our Lord Jesus Christ, we must prepare ourselves. What do I mean by that? Let me share what is on my heart.

A survey of a large Christian denomination's men reveals that only one in four men believe they are the spiritual leaders of their homes. Also, 41 percent of those men are occasionally attracted to pornography. These statistics do not please God. We must turn this around. We must be students of God's Word, which sets the standard for our behavior; we must conduct ourselves in a way that is pleasing to God, and be committed to holy living.

As men exit these Christian "main events", they are asking, "What's next?" I believe it is discipleship, evangelism, and Godly relationships. In order to do this, we must first purify our own lives and heal the areas that continuously take us into sin. We all experience a stronghold of some kind that needs our attention. It's different for everyone, but there is one common thread: obedience! Perhaps, however, I should say disobedience.

I had served my country and our presidents with honor, and now I serve my Lord Jesus with honor. I've gone from serving a President to serving a King – from "IN

THE LINE OF FIRE" to "in the line of holy fire." I have responded to God's call to grow godly men and raise an army of Christian men that are honorable in service to their Lord, families, communities, and churches…to raise up dead men!

A lot of men are thrust into the role of husband, father, or Christian man without the benefit of a good role model in their upbringing. The male image in the home was either nonexistent, or due to the drive to provide, there was an absence of leadership. It was delegated to the mother, to another sibling, or to no one at all. This has brought about a breakdown of respect for authority. There has been evidence of duplicity in the lives of our fathers.

We have become a generation that worships what we have and not who we are. The morals and accountability standards have lapsed into our desire to have our freedoms. Satan is having a great time as we self-indulge ourselves into the pit of hell.

This must change. God wants it to change. He has been pouring His Spirit out all over the country on men in an unprecedented way. He brought Promise Keepers to wake men up. A few years ago, He brought well over one million men to the mall in Washington, D.C., to repent for our sins of neglect in our communities, our country, and our families.

The men made a stand that day to take back the ground we allowed Satan to have. It is up to us to take it back and help guard that sacred ground for future generations. We must change ourselves so we can help shape an army – an army of God, marching into our homes, schools, churches, and communities to make a difference, putting flesh on dead bones.

If we continue putting garbage into our lives, then garbage will come out. We need to put the gospel into our lives, so the gospel will come out. God gave us a training manual to show us how to live our lives…His Word. He also sent His Holy Spirit to guide us in areas where we have not been trained. We only need to submit to His leading.

Obedience becomes the word of the day. We must obey what God has instructed us to do. This world can be very hard unless we totally depend on the Lord and His Word. We must be submitted and totally sold out to Christ. God is not asking for a 98 percent Christian. He wants – and will only take – a 100 percent Christian.

But it will takes a genuine change in the "status quo" way that we do things.

We need to set our standards according to God's, and resist the lure of Satan in our world today. God is calling men to offer a pleasing sacrifice to Him—a sacrifice of everything that we put ahead of Him, whether it be things or people. He wants us to stand before Him saying, "Yes, Lord, I will serve you. You are my Lord at any cost."

His Word gives us guideposts to live by. A Christian man:

1. Is a provider (1 Timothy 5:8)
2. Manages his household (1 Timothy 3:4,5,12)
3. Is submitted (Ephesians 5:21)
4. Is a covering (Ephesians 5:23)
5. Loves his wife as Christ loved the church (Ephesians 5:25)
6. Lifts up holy hands in prayer without anger or disputing (1 Timothy 2:8)

7. Does not break faith with his wife (Malachi 2:14-15)

8. Trains his children (Ephesians 6:4)

These are not all the Word teaches, but just some guideposts. A search of the Bible reveals much more. But that would mean a change of the natural order of things the world says are important to be successful.

Success, defined by God, would mean that we are reaching and bringing men closer to God.

What will it take to move men closer to God? Other men! Men reach men! But until we get it and become relational with men, we will continue to struggle. We need to change the way we think. We need to focus!

I wasn't always this focused. I evolved or changed. Prior to starting Champions of Honor as a trans-denominational approach of ministry to men, I served as the leader of a national denominational ministry to men called HonorBound: Men of Promise. Prior to that, I was "Mr. Secret Service" doing my duty for God and country. But as we let God in our lives we continue to evolve! What was – is not anymore. As we evolve with God, our focus shifts and our dead bones become alive!

So what will it take to be men focused upon God? We must be involved in a circle of Champions that keeps us focused on men and God.

God showed me one day on the way to work what this means. I was on a three-mile bridge and within the first mile, God spoke to me and said **"If you focus, you will finish."** Before I finished the second mile, He said **"If you focus on the finish, you will finish strong."** Before I could complete the third mile of the bridge, He said, **"If**

you finish strong, others will finish with you!"

Too many men are focused on the wrong things or wrong programs. Understanding our Biblical roots of masculinity will help us know our destiny with God.

What will it take to change you? What will it take to change a world? Men need to remain focused on God and their circle of champions. Champions change; if not, you stagnate.

Change realigns our focus. Change gives us a different approach. Change keeps us growing. Change matures our soul. Change gives us hope.

Are you willing to change your lifestyle to conform to what God expects of each one of us? Remember, change is good! Are you ready for a change in your life?

1. Where is your focus?
2. Do you really know Him?
3. What kind of role models did you have growing up?
4. How did they affect you for change?
5. Are you prepared to change from concentration on self to concentration on God and family?
6. Do you manage your household in God's way?
7. How do you change your status quo life?
8. Are you ready for change?
9. Where is your focus?

CHAPTER 4

OVERCOMING...
Bad Seed

Incorrigible. According to the dictionary it means "unable to be reformed or changed; a delinquent."

While rarely used, the word has special meaning for me because it was the stamp placed on my Boy Scout's file when I was kicked out of the boy's program at age 11. They determined that I was a "bad seed" and I was corrupting the other boys. They saw my delinquency and their inability to control me as something they did not want to deal with. In their wisdom, they decided that Chuck Brewster was "unreachable" and "unworthy" of their time.

This is not the best record for a career United States Secret Service Agent and now the leader of a National Men's Network. What happened? Were they wrong? If so, what lesson can be learned?

I am not suggesting to you that I was an angel. I probably deserved some of the labels I received. I was difficult and wild, but I realize now it was not because I was unreachable. It was because no one had ever reached out to me as a fatherless child in need of guidance from a Biblical perspective.

At the age of three, my Father was killed in an automobile accident in Florida. Nine years later my mother re-married, but he turned out to be an abusive alcoholic who did not like kids. I had to learn early to fend for myself for there was no strong male influence in my life. My mother did constantly affirm me, but she worked full time; so many times I was left on my own. In fact, my mother had to move across the street from the elementary school so I could walk to school because I kept missing the bus. Even then the truant officer knew me by my first name.

My mother was wonderful and I felt her love and affirmation loud and clear. She went the extra mile to make sure I knew I was a winner, but it was not with a father's blessing.

My early Boy Scout leaders would be shocked to find out that Law Enforcement was my chosen profession, let alone becoming one of the leaders of the Secret Service. Thank goodness juvenile records are not public record or there would have been a tale of how I was charged as a 17 year old with contributing to the delinquency of minors (alcohol on the beach of Pensacola).

Now, I am the leader of international ministry to men… incorrigible? No one is unreachable when the Holy Spirit is involved. No matter how "dead" a man may be, through the Holy Spirit, he can be risen! I was one such man.

As a Secret Service Agent, we were trained to train others. If at any moment, I would be unable to fulfill my duty due to an injury or another problem, someone else was there and trained to complete the mission. I had to mentor and train those under me to do what was necessary to bring about the mission of the agency. As a father and a husband, I determined that I would not allow my children to grow up with any labels that would prevent them from being what God wanted them to be. No matter what anyone else thought, my children would always be reachable in my mind.

After Chad and Lanie were born, I realized that I really didn't know exactly how to be a dad. With no healthy models growing up, I was not sure what I needed to do or how I needed to act. I just knew that no matter what would come their way they were reachable. They must know that I was there with them no matter what would happen.

Am I perfect? Far from it! I remember telling my children that I did not have a clue on how to be a great dad. I told them to remember the good things and forget the bad things when they raise their children. I might lose my temper, yell, and make wrong decisions, but I will never let them feel unreachable, because they are reachable. As they have grown up we have had our moments, sometimes they can be rebellious and I can be pig-headed. But ultimately I have the responsibility of moving towards my children, because they are reachable.

Like my family and the Secret Service Agents I mentored, God has placed on my heart to mentor and train men, to help breathe life into men. Just like in the Service, there needs to be other men who can step into the battle with the enemy and take our place. It is our responsibility to pour into the lives of other men and train them to do battle. Though they may not have had healthy models growing up, we can mentor them. It is not their responsibility to reach out to us, it is our responsibility to reach out to them. Jesus gave us the Great Commission, not the Great Reception. Each of us must determine that the men around us are reachable. They may not look like us. They may not always agree with us. But they are God's children and no one in the Kingdom of God is unreachable. No one gets kicked out of our community of faith because they are "incorrigible." With God, all things are possible!

This is why we need Champions for God, helping others fulfill their destiny. This needs to be fivefold in our approach as Champions. We need to be *Apostolic* in fathering a fatherless generation, and *Prophetic* by speaking into the lives of those we are mentoring. We also need to be *Teachers* helping to explain the hidden truths of life and *Pastoral* in our nurturing approach. Finally, we need to be *Evangelistic* in our approach of others to help them see the hope of trusting God.

1. How do you personally overcome a part of your past that might not be good?
2. How do you try to overcome your imperfections?
3. Do you practice, "With God all things are possible!"?
4. How does the five-fold ministry work through your life?

CHAPTER 5

RE-FATHER...
America

If we look at the condition of the families in America we could assume we need to put a man into every home and that would be a solution for the absent father condition in this nation. With 39.6 % of the children in America going to bed every night without their biological father in the home, this would be a possible solution. But, that is not what I am referring to in my statement that we need to *"Re-Father America"*.

Over the last three decades, I have concluded that most of the social ills of America lies within the absent father or the father vacuum condition within the hearts of men <u>and</u> women, as much as their children. The lack of affirmation of a father or a man has negatively affected the family and thus the nation. If we go further and say the absence of a godly father, the statistics would be much higher. This has caused social anarchy in our family structure and is confusing to the rest of the world.

Lawsuits are constantly filed to take away "Under God" from our nation's pledge, prayers, and from all settings. I wonder how empty the motto, "One Nation Under God" seems to the millions of immigrants that migrate to this nation. I am surprised that we are still called a Judeo-Christian nation. In fact, if any of the presidential candidates started affirming God and declaring this a Judeo-Christian nation; they would feel the heat of the media and special interest groups. No, we are a "people-pleasing" nation. We respond to polls that try to please the largest voting groups.

Actually, the United States has become "Many Nations under Many gods" and that is the problem. A more accurate description is "Many Nations Under Money", or "Many Nations Under Political Correctness", and possibly "Many Nations Under Personal Choices". We don't want to offend anyone so we strive to be bland, apathetic and without passion for a living and most real God.

There is no doubt that everyone would like families to work together and stay together, but when God is missing and work or personal pleasure has taken His place, then we will never have the solid family foundations that this nation once enjoyed. "One Nation Under God" is a motto that was lived out in each family in a community. There was a sense of community and God was the center. That is not the case today. I don't care how many Christian television shows, churches, or compassion ministries are in our cities, the vast majority of people have been lulled into a dangerous sense of complacency that allows the devil to rob, kill and destroy in an unprecedented way.

Most are afraid to speak out in the public political arena for fear of being branded a "Right Wing Christian Zealot".

Maybe that is what we need? People to speak out and be labeled.

Jesus said in Matthew 12:30, "He who is not with me is against me, and he who does not gather with me scatters." We need to stand for God and speak for Him in our nation, without fear!

Re-fathering America is not to bring men into each

home, but to bring <u>Father God</u> into each home. When we have begun to do this, then maybe we can be called " One Nation Under God" once again.

I ask YOU to join me to take on this gigantic goal to *"Reach Every Family in America, One Man at a Time"*. Experience has shown that if you reach a man for Jesus, he will, in turn, reach his entire family over 90% of the time. That is a strong statement when compared to children being successful only 3.5% of the time and women only 17% of the time.

If we are systematic in our approach and use the Word of God to challenge men to grow in Christ, they will respond. It is when we try to reach and grow men through the world that we have failed. Challenging men to be "<u>Champions</u>" and to make a stand for God is a masculine way to reach a nation.

As a champion, empowered by the Holy Spirit, you need to be equipped as "Ministers to Men" in their neighborhoods, workplace, and communities and sent out as a vast Army of Champions to conquer a decadent society led by men who do not walk with God.

Once men stand up for God in a society, then families will change and a nation will change. But it is a man-to-man battlefield. It has to be fought one battle at a time. Just like David, the Champion for the Army of God, against Goliath the Champion for the Philistines, men must equip themselves with the weapons that are natural to them and use the skill God has given us, and we need to clothe ourselves in our own armor provided by God and not the armor of others like when Saul tried to offer David his armor. David recognized he could not fight in someone else's armor. David was successful because he had his focus on God and his faith was in God. God had developed him for this battle.

Champions are made, not born! Join us today as we attempt to "Re-Father a Nation"!

1. What kind of a father are you?
2. When your children think of you, what do they think of?
3. Are you a Godly representative to your wife and children?
4. What do you do specifically to bring Father God into your home?

CHAPTER 6

RESTORE...
America's Family

Why is it that when we think of the "Family," it brings up an image of the Godfather or some television sitcom? The core American family has become dependent on the television for direction and guidance. The television is the barometer for the health of the family. Our youth are judged by what they say on television news, our marriage by what is on the latest soap opera or talk show. We are basing our family values on the Television and not God's Word. We live in a surreal state most of the time, thinking to ourselves that we will strike gold somehow or achieve some secular success that will complete our identity.

Champions are focused upon reaching America's youth and the American family. The truth is that in order to reach America's youth we are going to have to find America's families. At the rate the family is disintegrating, there will be no families left in the future. We have already seen the decline of the male in the home with 40% of our homes in a fatherless condition. Lionel Tiger in his book "Decline of the Males" has said that we don't need the males anymore. With science we can impregnate the females, government can provide subsistence and the female can grow the species. He called this new family unit a "Bureaugomy", a mother, child, and bureaucrat.

Some radical people say that man is not necessary. We have bought this trash and believe it because of television and/or minority positions of politically correct men that have a guilt trip for their treatment of women in the past. The absolute truth is that we no longer believe in the "Absolute Truth," God's Word. If we are to believe God's Word, then we know that men have a unique responsibility to the family.

In the <u>USA TODAY</u>, June 7, 2000, was an article entitled <u>"Absent Dads Scar Millions of Daughters for Life."</u> This news story was about Jonetta Rose Barras, a Washington D.C. columnist and author of a newly released book *"Whatever Happened to Daddy's Little Girl? The Impact of Fatherlessness on Black Women."* Barras outlines the impact of the abandonment of the family by the father especially felt by little girls:

- The "Un" factor, feeling unworthy and unloved;
- The "triple fear factor", fear of rejection, abandonment, and commitment;
- The "sexual healing factor" women hoping to be healed by physical closeness;
- The "over factor", the need to over-compensate, over-achieve and over-saturate to gain acceptance or show what the father has missed;
- Finally the "RAD factor," rage, anger, depression.

Barras says that "acknowledging our loss (of the father) permits the opportunity for us to grieve" and "if there is no forgiveness of her parents, especially her father, then there can be no moving on to her future."

According to Barras, "Fathers teach girls how to relate to men and maneuver in a male dominated society; become comfortable as to who they are as a girl and later as a woman; they help you negotiate in the real world."

"If it is true that a father helps to develop his daughter's confidence in herself and in her femininity; that he helps her to shape her style and understanding of male-female bonding; and that he introduces her to the external world, plotting navigational courses for her success, then surely it is an indisputable conclusion that the absence of these lessons can produce a severely wounded and disabled woman," she writes.

We have always heard how important it is for a father to shape the character of his sons, but it is equally important to shape the character of his daughters. Columnist William Raspberry of the <u>WASHINGTON POST</u> writes: "With sons, fathers know it's their job to set examples of male behavior and to talk to their boys about how to be men. And we think therefore that the moms should tell the daughters about becoming a woman." But he says, "Fathers need to model behavior and a set of expectations so our daughters know how to spot a good man when they see one."

Raspberry concludes, "When fathers are absent, our daughters miss out on some incredibly important insights into how men are, can be, ought to be." He continues with "I'm not saying that if the dads are not around, girls can't grow up to be self-confident. I'm simply saying that when dads – wholesome dads – are around, it's a lot easier for girls to have a good sense of themselves and not feel themselves unworthy of love and respect."

I find it interesting that the secular world and even the "liberal" news media cannot get away from the absolute truth of the Word of God. Even though these writers are not saying it in Christian terms, what they are saying are Christian truths. We should be models as Christ was a model for us, we should forgive those that have offended us, we should entrust to reliable men to teach others, we should live the life according to the plan that God has laid out for us in His Bible.

Why have so many of our families broken apart? The main reason is they have not been held together by a committed father. A father who has the fear, love, compassion, and discipline of the Lord. Too many men have walked away from their spiritual responsibility as fathers and men.

Many have not risen to the level of being a true "champion" in the eyes of their children and spouse. What can we do to repair this wall of division and destruction? We must repent, repair, and restore the damage caused by our unfaithfulness in our duty as men. We must be fathers to the fatherless, mentoring and restoring lives according to the Word. We must turn our hearts to the children and the hearts of our children to the fathers less we are struck with a curse.

But where are the men?

Men are in the Workplace…Where Else?

We men love to work. We spend hours upon hours planning our workday. We strategize our growth in the workplace and build a campaign to succeed in our work endeavors. As a young man we educate or train ourselves so that we are marketable and then we start "making our bones" in the marketplace. A lot of times we neglect everything else in order to nurture our "position" at work. We are consumed with making our mark in life.

That sure paints a pretty bad picture if it is not balanced with a home and family life that is quality and important to us. We have been told to build in some quality family time or if we are single to allow with some quality personal time building our bodies or just relaxing.

Wow, that is a pretty busy schedule! When does God show up in our priorities? Actually, as men, we should be striving to build our relationship with God _**first**_...before work, before family, and before ourselves. If we put as much time in developing our spiritual lives as we do our workplace image, just imagine the growth in our personal journey with God. Just imagine how our children would respect us more?

As we begin to develop a relationship with God, we can't help but be convinced that we need to share this relationship with others. The Word says to go and be witnesses, but we feel that we are weak in this area. That is because we do not put in the time like we do for our "profession" so is relegated to being a hobby...or even less. We get our church fix on Sunday but the rest of the week we spend cultivating our worldly endeavors.

Have I hit home yet! I have for me. I was like that in my early days and can be that way now in ministry if I do not give God the first fruits of my life.

When I meet with businessmen I cannot relate totally with them on the ups and downs of the business marketplace, as my first career was government service. I can relate some because I have investigated men in the marketplace that have taken the illegal road to success. This does not make me an expert in the marketplace, but I can relate to the managerial and leadership issues of the business world.

I learned a life lesson from my mentor, Father God, early in my life. Keep my nose to the grindstone. Do the right thing. Later in my life I realized what this means: Develop a good relationship with God and apply it to everything you do. Don't just do things and then go to God to get approval but work with Him to bring all the endeavors of your life into the full impact of a Christian life experience.

The bottom line…We need to focus on God first, spend adequate time with Him to help develop all other areas of our life. Build a life plan that involves our family and work around His mentorship. Don't forget that men need other men to help shape that godly plan!

Don't isolate yourself or have your "church" friends and "work" friends segregated. By integrating both worlds God will use you to help shape a life plan in others. God wants you to be a Champion, as you help to restore your family.

1. What do you purposefully do to spend more time with your family?
2. What do you do, as head of your household, to draw more attention to each other, instead of the television?
3. How do you react in a family situation…in kindness or rage?
4. How do you teach your kids to relate to others in the real world?
5. What positive difference do you make in your workplace?
6. How do you nurture a quality family time?
7. How do you apply your personal relationship with God to everything you do?

CHAPTER 7

FITNESS...
An Essential Ingredient of Being a Christian

Are you "Fit" to be a Christian?

In all my years in law enforcement fitness was an essential ingredient to staying alive. If you were not able to perform the job, you might die. If you were not mentally, physically, and even emotionally prepared, you were expendable and deemed useless in your position.

While serving in the United States Secret Service I realized the importance that the agency put on physical conditioning and readiness for battle based upon those early days. We trained relentlessly for weeks to be prepared for any situation and any circumstance that we may encounter. Putting an unprepared and unqualified man to guard the President of the United States is foolishness. Therefore, through training and testing we were sifted like wheat. It was only through the demands of training that we were able to find out who was fit to go to the next level. I also realized through experiences such as the day President Reagan was shot, that you can never over prepare in order to be ready in season and out.

It is like that today in ministry, you need to prepare for the battle and be ready for anything the enemy throws at you. Luke 22:31-32 says, "Simon, Simon, Satan has asked to sift you as wheat. But, I have prayed for you, Simon that your faith may not fail." God allows us to encounter temptation and trials, but within certain limitations. Your confidence and strength needs to rest in the Lord, but you need to do all you can do to be the man God has called you to be, in order that you can "strengthen your brothers" (Luke 22:32b).

As I travel and speak to diverse cultures of men, I notice that there is an underlying issue in just about every man I meet. I frequently ask men what their father was like when they were growing up. The responses I get vary but the majority of men seem to have numerous issues stemming from the absent, abusive, or neglectful dad. I wonder how prepared we are to face the world when we have not been prepared properly by our dad's? As you grow up it is like a training ground and you reflect the atmosphere you are exposed to. Thus the command in Proverbs 22:6 that says, ***"Train up a child in the way he should go, and when he is old he will not turn from it."***

This command is directed to parents, more specifically, to the fathers. Our youth is the training period for life. Our coach needs to be our dad. Unfortunately, many of us did not have an atmosphere that was a proper and godly training ground. So we reproduce the vacuum we grew up in. We want to change, but we have not filled the void of our childhood.

Many homes today are not prepared for the world as it has evolved because we never went through the proper training camp. We as Christian men need to help train those who have not been trained by showing and revealing the love of our Father God. As families are torn apart by divorce, abandonment or just no marriage at all, the church must be prepared, physically and spiritually, to fill that void. It cannot be done as usual but must be a supernatural act of God.

Men and women of today are birthing babies in a genderless society and to say we can bring a dad to every home is not reasonable. But, we can be models and we can reflect the love of a Father in Heaven that is a Father to the fatherless. We have to begin to turn the children's hearts, young and old, to the Father.

The only way we can do this is by conditioning ourselves to be physically, mentally, and spiritually "Fit" so we are ready in season and out! To be a champion means that you are also to be "fit!"

1. How fit are you, both physically and spiritually?
2. How do you overcome any issues that you may have had with your own father?
3. Who have you forgiven lately, and why?
4. Are you really "fit" to be a dad or a good husband?
5. No one is perfect, but you are still a champion, so what do you do to fill any void in your life, or the lives of your children or spouse?

CHAPTER 8

OBEYING...
The Ten Commandments

The only way a true Army of God can be raised, is to have champions to obey His laws and His commandments.

A few years ago, we witnessed a great battle by Judge Roy Moore and his display of the Ten Commandments in the rotunda of the Alabama Supreme Court. His contention is that the Commandments are the basis of law for the free world. I watched as the ACLU used those laws to remove the Commandments from display and having it upheld by the courts so that Judge Moore was the one who was censured.

After reading Exodus 20: 1-17, the scriptures as given by God to Moses, I reached a conclusion that we should not proudly display them since we do not obey them. America with all of our proclamations to be "One Nation Under God" – is Not!

Let's examine each commandment:

1. "I am the Lord your God...you shall have no other gods before me"

2. "You shall not make for yourself an idol in the form of anything..."

3. "You shall not misuse the name of the Lord your God..."

4. "Remember the Sabbath by keeping it holy..."

5. "Honor your father and your mother..."

6. "You shall not murder."

7. "You shall not commit adultery."

8. "You shall not steal."

9. "You shall not give false testimony against your neighbor."

10. "You shall not covet your neighbor's house…wife… servants…belongings…"

In America today tell me which one of the above we obey.

(1) We have gods in our lives in the form of jobs, football, fishing, and self or family (kids) just to name a few. We put these things before God.

(2) We produce numerous symbols to worship, not the least would be the Dollar Bill.

(3) We use the Lord's name in vain so much it is on prime time television.

(4) The Sabbath is just another day and is not set aside for any meaning except personal pleasure.

(5) We do not honor our father and mother. The father is absent in most homes in America if not physically most assuredly spiritually.

(6) We kill unborn babies daily and call it pro choice instead of pro death.

(7) Pornography and lust have consumed our thought live and fueled by the advertising world. Sex outside the marriage covenant is rampant in our nation.

(8) We think nothing of swindling our neighbor if it will turn a bigger profit. Just look at the number of companies that steal from hard working Americans.

(9) It is nothing in this land to talk about people and condemn them even though our facts are not true or only half true. It is called Gossip and it is everywhere, in church and out.

(10) We constantly try to live up to our neighbor's standards instead of Gods. We desire what they have and we strive to attain it.

So when we talk about displaying the Ten Commandments, let us first talk about demonstrating them in our own lives. It is not proper to display something we do not believe. It only becomes another idol, which violates the second commandment.

Judge Roy Moore took a stand, but what needs to happen is that the people of this nation need to take a stand. We need to "Stand Firm in our Faith!" then the Ten Commandments will be displayed in our actions and our hearts.

1. Are you ready to take a stand?
2. Do you really obey all of the Ten Commandments?
3. What "gods" in your life are unhealthy, time-wise?
4. How do you not let the love of money to try to consume you and your family?
5. Look again at each of the Ten Commandments, how do you demonstrate that you are obeying each one?

CHAPTER 9

ETHICAL...
in an Unethical World

As far back as the beginning of civilization there have been unethical acts against the laws of the culture. Man has not invented anything new in the last few years; it is something we have been doing for a long time, deceiving others for personal gain or favor. But why has there been such an increase in recent days of unethical and otherwise illegal business practices?

We read the headlines about companies like Enron, WorldCom, and others, involved in inflating the worth and taking huge profits while the company and employees suffer losses. There have always been those who believe in something because greed or wanting to be in on something successful just blinds their judgment. I have investigated fraud schemes most of my adult life.

It can always be said that if it is too good to be true, then it is not true! But the growth and publicity of the lifestyle of the rich and famous has brought greed to every sector of our communities, and the church is no exception. We strive to keep up or out do our neighbors.

Greed has become a sin of extraordinary size in the current affluent status of this nation. This has to be addressed for things have not always been this way. In days of old, your reputation was important in business and unethical dealings would be summarily rejected in the business and public arena. But in today's world, it seems that being unethical is a business practice that helps create a positive bottom line, after all that is all it's about, the profit margin!

There is a non-tangible asset called "good will" that is assessed when looking at a company. The "good will" needs to appear on the surface as a positive asset in business. It is even assigned a worth when purchasing a business. To falsify the "good will" is an act of deceit. Even in the church "good will" comes into play. We want people to think well of our church and we put on our best face every Sunday. But, what are you looking like on Monday, Tuesday, or the rest of the week.

Being ethical starts at home, goes with us to church, and applies in our chosen profession. But if we are not ethical at home, not teaching our children ethics, and not applying them to our everyday lives; then how do we expect any different outcome than what we see today. The breakdown is not the "Business World"...it is in the "Family World." We are deceiving our loved ones at home, church and community, then applying the same tactics at work. Years ago the family was strong and being ethical in business was strong also. Business has not failed, our family lifestyles have. Dead men need to rise up above the unethical battles, both at home and at work.

So how do we change this trend and insulate our families to remain ethical as a Christian in today's business and church settings?

There are some simple steps to remaining ethical in an unethical world, but it means self-sacrifice. If you are willing, some of these steps are:

1. Put God first in your life and leave Him there. Don't have your Sunday face and then return to your business on

Monday and look like the world.

2. Fast and pray for your family, business, and your employees.

3. Be transparent with other godly men in an accountable relationship.

4. Tithe on your business gross, and support ministry endeavors within your business and community. Your blessing will return blessings.

5. Stand fast when others would flee. Conform to the Word, not the world.

6. Leave a legacy in your family and profession that reflects godly character.

7. Give God the credit in everything, lest you boast of your strength and abilities.

Many more can be added to the list. There is no easy way out. It is hard work to remain ethical in an unethical world. The pressures are tremendous to succeed at whatever the cost. But, is it worth an eternity of damnation and a failed legacy in your family?

I am asking you to be a truly Christian businessman… committed to God, his family, his community, and his church. Form a team to Rise–Up and fight off the enemy that wants to undermine our ethics and our legacy.

1. Do you ever cheat on anything?
2. Do you promote high ethics within your family?
3. How will others judge you for your "good will"?
4. What do you do to insulate your family from unethical friends?
5. How do you remain ethical in an unethical world?

CHAPTER 10

LEADERSHIP...
Going Where God Leads

I see ministry <u>by</u> men in our churches, but not ministry <u>to</u> men. I see dry and dead bones. As men receive true ministry in our churches, and the breath of the Holy Spirit, men will be resurrected into true champions.

I realize the need to bring men home from the "stadium events" and involve them back into the church. Men need to be disciplined and engaged in multiplying themselves, especially if one is to become a true leader. God wants His men to literally "carry the ball" and bring genuine repentance to this great country.

Building Brothers president Dan Schaffer once asked me a question that resonated in my soul, "Is growing men to spiritual maturity foundational for the church?"

I was already in a reflective and God-seeking frame of mind as I pondered this question. I started realizing the importance of growing godly men is linked to bringing revival to men in our nation.

I have seen much in the past several years. Being relatively new to ministry, I had a lot to learn. I didn't want to learn from man. I wanted to learn from God. I wanted to see a broader move of God in our nation on men and I wanted God to move more in my own life. I believe seeking God and His direction are the only way to focus any ministry.

We have focused our ministry to men toward a time of intimate worship of God, extended time at the altar in the presence of God, and training to be powerful men of God through male-oriented discipleship materials.

I realize that even though God was moving among men, there is still an attitude that men's ministries is just another of the many ministries in the church; and every ministry needs equal time. Equal time is a truly democratic American ideal deeply ingrained in our lives. Church leaders continue to view men's ministries as a pancake breakfast or an event for men to attend, instead of a foundational issue for the local church.

We have tried to attract men to our churches with secular events and classes such as sporting events or classes on how to manage money. But in today's world, we need to challenge our men with spiritual growth in worship, discipleship, and multiplication.

A church led by men who have a renewed sense of spiritual worth will revolutionize a local church body and the community it resides within. When a man's heart is changed, his hands will soon follow. He wants to do something because men are "doers." We have to meet man's "doing" need as well as his spiritual growth. It takes a balance of both needs. A balanced ministry to men is both inwardly and outwardly focused.

When true ministry takes place in a man's life, he will change. He will be led by God to become a valiant leader for his family and his church. Being a leader is not a torch that every man desires to carry, but it is a torch we must carry. The only way we can dare to dream of a day where men are the leaders in their home is to equip them, encourage them, and release them into being the leader that God has called them to be.

This process does not happen overnight. Take Joseph for example. Here was a man who dreamed of leadership. He believed that God had created him to be a strong and mighty leader, even within his own home. The journey that led him to fulfilling this destiny was not easy and by no means brief. It was a long and difficult adventure that was filled with false accusations, imprisonment, and rejection.

There are a number of times within Joseph's life that he could have easily given up and quit; but he chose to trust and place his faith in God. The result, found in Genesis 41-47, speaks for itself.

As men, we need to stand firm on the promise that God has called us to become leaders. More times than we would like to admit, though, we shutter at the thought of our potential as a leader and then chalk it up to a simple lack of faith. Nothing could be further from the truth. Jesus said that if we have faith even the size of a mustard seed. In case you are not up on your botany, a mustard seed is quite small. So it is safe to say that we do not have a faith problem, but rather a doubting problem.

Doubt is a key tool of the enemy to discourage and depress a man from standing up and being God's leader to his family and to his church. We need to recognize this in our lives and ask God to remove it.

Today's deepest needs are within the family. Some attention is being paid to the deteriorating condition of the family, but not enough. We are not looking at the root cause nor willing to address the father vacuum and the enormous problems that arise from this vacuum. It takes leaders who are willing to address this issue and make a stance to reverse the pendulum of the father vacuum.

As I travel and speak across this nation, I am constantly faced with men who are weeping at the altar from the effects of their fatherless vacuum. I believe the long-term effects of fatherless homes have caused untold numbers of divorces, abuse, and lives full of hidden sin. Shockingly, most of these men are a part of active churches, but hide their sin. I realized the fatherless issue in their lives left a hole that could not be filled except when they dealt with it, in total submission to God – grabbing hold of the Father and finding a resting place in His love.

We can only be a Champion and a good leader when we submit to God, totally, 100 percent.

We need to realize that men's ministry, as a foundational issue for the church, has crumbled from the stress of the world surrounding it. The pressure for men to succeed for the sake of their families or their own selfish interests has removed men from the godly leadership needed in their homes and churches.

We have succumbed to the secular world in addressing the needs of the church, instead of getting back to the basics in the Bible and applying biblical truths to our everyday lives. As you embrace biblical truths, you are putting flesh on your dry bones.

I urge you to attempt to break free from this downward spiral by the power of the Holy Spirit and return to face-to-face interaction with God. We are continuing to point men to God and not to a ministry or program. Following God is not a Sunday thing, it's an everyday thing.

1. How disciplined are you every day?
2. What do you purposefully do to add to your spiritual maturity in Christ?
3. What do you do to take your "Men's Ministry" into your everyday lifestyle?
4. Do you have the marking for a true leader?
5. Do you effectively lead in your home?
6. How do you follow God in your everyday life?

CHAPTER 11

FELLOWSHIP...
A Good Thing

Choosing to fellowship with God is each man's responsibility. God made us for fellowship. He also gave us the free will to choose to fellowship. Choosing not to fellowship doesn't negate our responsibilities, but when we choose another way, we lose God's leadership and guidance.

Every man must choose whom he will serve. He must decide how he is going to live his life. Unfortunately, most men choose not to choose. Instead, they simply ride it out to see how it plays out. They let parents, bosses, wives, children, or friends guide them through life. Their indecision causes a ripple effect on the lives under their responsibility – their families. Friends just see these men as "good ol' boys" but not men after God's own heart and thus influencing others towards Christ.

Why do men fail to choose to fellowship with God? I have found that men are busy having fun while being a good man. They see taking a step towards God as losing the freedom of the good life they enjoy. They don't mind being good and probably moral men, but to be godly men, would require changing their entire lives.

John Eldredge in his book, *Wild at Heart*, writes, "The problem with men, we are told, is that we don't know how to keep our promises, be spiritual leaders, talk to our wives or girlfriends, or raise our children. But if we try really hard, we can reach the lofty summit of becoming a nice guy. That's what we hold up as a model of Christian maturity: Really Nice Guys!"

Eldredge continues to say that this dedication to niceness is the reason there are so many tired and lonely women, so many fatherless children, and so few men around. "We've taken away the dreams of a man's heart and told him to play the man. Or as C.S. Lewis said, 'We castrate the gelding and bid him be fruitful.'"

My friend Dan Schaffer wrote, "If you want to know the priority in a man's heart, look at his calendar and checkbook." He spends his time and money on what impacts him and his desires. Dan believes, as do I, that developing a man to spiritual maturity is foundational to the church. Our example is Jesus. He invested his entire ministry developing the disciples.

Somehow we lost that priority and the church became feminized. Men's ministry became what men did and not who they are. We did not minister to our men and hold them accountable. We enlisted them as ushers and other service models for the church. We made them "Really Nice Guys."

Along came this masculine revolution called Promise Keepers and changed the way men were behaving towards Christ. We actually got excited again to be in relationship with God. We had a lot of baggage to straighten out. Since our pastors were also going through changes, they did not understand us.

The problem is that men don't really want to be "nice guys." They see this as a feminine view of a man. Men want the respect of other men and to be perceived as a virile man, a strong man. The main them of John Eldredge's book is that "Deep in his heart, every man longs for a battle to fight, an adventure to live, and a beauty to rescue." God made us that way and it is unnatural to behave any other way. Without this affirmation we do not feel we are men – true men.

This nation needs godly men! We need godly fathers and husbands! We must choose to follow God while keeping our masculine instincts, but lose the sin nature of man. Being a godly man means:

• We have a battle to fight. The enemy of sin in our own lives.

• We have an adventure to live – guiding our families and friends toward a relationship with God.

• We have a damsel to rescue – our wives and daughters kept free from the captivity of sin.

God sent John the Baptist to introduce the world to Jesus. He chose a man who clearly proclaimed Jesus through his words and deeds. But John was a man with a relationship with God and a responsibility to declare the coming of his Lord.

"There came a man who was sent from God…he came as a testimony…so that through him all men might believe." (John 1:6-7).

John the Baptist knew his purpose in life. He was called to live and speak in such a way that the people of his day would believe in Jesus. God continues to issue the call for man who will testify in word and deed so their families and a new generation will believe.

If these principles are put into practice, people will meet Jesus, one new believer at a time. This is a way to ignite and unite the men of the Church to fulfill their calling

– starting today!

We have a battle to fight, an adventure to live, and a beauty to rescue.

With our rudder into the deep waters of God, we will move in the right directions when the storms of life appear. We will hold the course set because of our fellowship with God. But our rudder must be deep. As champions in the Army of God, our feet must be firmly planted. It cannot be superficial; else we will be blown in the wrong direction.

Todd Beamer had his rudder deep into God's waters. He was a promise keeper before there were Promise Keepers. He was a good husband, a good friend, and a good father. He was grounded in God's Word and taught it at his church. When a storm came to United Airlines Flight 93, September 11, 2001, Todd was ready! He was like any other man on his way to work, providing for his family, but in one second, the enemy showed up and Todd had to make a choice.

As Todd sat in his seat while terrorists commandeered the aircraft, he could have sat still and watched evil accomplish its plan. Instead, Todd put his rudder deep into God's waters and sprang into action. He was a man with a battle to fight, an adventure to live, and a damsel to rescue.

Todd assessed the situation.

Todd gathered like-minded men---like being in Fellowship.

Todd asked God for help.

Finally, Todd overcame his enemy.

Todd's last words were, "Are you guys ready? Let's roll!" We're sounding the call to confront the evil in our world.

We are asking men all over America the same question: "Are we ready guys? Let's roll!"

1. In making a decision to serve God, are you really doing that, really?
2. What about your time, are you "too busy doing even good things" to take enough time for personal relationship and communication with God?
3. Look at your checkbook and calendar. Now try to understand your personal priorities in life?
4. How do you follow God, while maintaining your masculine instincts?
5. What battle do you fight in this life?
6. What victories have you achieved?
7. Are you really grounded in your faith?

CHAPTER 12

HEARING...
God's Voice

Do you hear from God every day?

Does your spiritual walk open up the heavenly airwaves?

In our daily walk, we need to hear from God. Relying on our past experiences or our own strength causes us to miss what He has for us today.

God does not walk away from us. He is great and mighty. He can talk to each of us at the same time. Can you even imagine the greatness of God?

God is speaking to men. The Holy Spirit is breathing life into former "dead men." Once dry bones are now filled with purpose after hearing from God. My heart's cry is that you will listen to God, so He can speak to you, personally.

Are you hearing His voice? He wants to have a personal conversation with us each day. He loved the fellowship He experienced with Adam in the Garden. He desires that same fellowship with you. Sometimes our prayers are simply a catalog list of our needs, but we all need to take time daily to "wait on the Lord." He will speak loudly to us in the quiet of our spirit.

As we enter into times of prayer, we must train ourselves to listen. Conversations with self-centered, talkative people are difficult. They make it hard to get a word in. Those individuals have an even harder time listening. Sometimes we act that way with God. We list our needs. We have our routine or ritual – and then we say, "Amen."

Take time to listen to God. He has something to say. Meditate on His Word. Open your ears and hear what He is saying. Ask God to let you feel with His heart, see with His eyes, and hear with His ears. The world around you will seem different.

As I listen to His voice, I continue to see the breakdown of our society and the rampant rise in violent acts. I can't help but wonder, "Where is God?" Did we leave Him behind in our churches and homes? No, God is there, but we aren't listening to His voice. We, the men of America, must start paying attention to what God is saying.

I believe God is telling us to take a stand for Him! It is time for the men in America to ARISE and declare, "As for me and my house, we will serve the Lord."

We often go to church to worship Jesus. We should bring Jesus to church with us. Jesus is with us all the time, not waiting at church for us to come and worship Him or pray or reflect on His goodness. He must be visible in our lives at work at home, to our neighbor, and everywhere we go. He needs to live in us. We must be consumed by Him, living every moment for His soon-coming return, spreading the Gospel with the fervor of a sports fanatic.

"Sons of God" we need to ARISE! I have seen men come alive in events around the nation, but that is not enough. We need to be alive in Christ every waking moment. We don't have one Jesus for Sunday morning and another for Monday or Tuesday. We need to take Jesus with us at all times to share His love in the marketplace and in our communities.

It is my prayer and earnest desire that YOU will be

used by God to raise up a nation of men committed to wholeheartedly serving God---sold out men of God who lead their homes and serve their churches.

But it all starts out with you, as you listen to the voice of God. Hearing from Him will give you divine instructions for the day!

How do you hear from God?

When is your time with Him? Many people talk to God in different ways, but listening is the key.

I recently visited some churches in Korea. They are desperate for God. Prayer and waiting on God is a divine thing. In churches when they start praying, there is a bell to say pause and listen. The prayers are intense and the phrases are reflective. Champions listen to their coach. Let the Holy Spirit be your coach.

1. Do you hear from God every day?
2. Does your spiritual walk open up the heavenly airwaves?
3. Do you take time every day to listen for His voice?
4. Do you receive "divine direction" for your decisions you make every day?
5. How does God instruct you?

CHAPTER 13

ATTACK...
The Walls of Sin

Are you too content and too comfortable?

Are you ready for a "Holy War?"

Across our nation, people are reeling from the catastrophic acts that impacted our country and the free world. Within the midst of chaotic and troublesome times since September 11th, we have had to ask ourselves, "Are we ready for what lies ahead?"

People everywhere are crying out to God in an unprecedented way. Immediately after 9-11, churches were full, people were getting saved, and unity was in abundance once again in our nation.

But soon apathy set in. Our comfortable lifestyles again took control of our thoughts. I pray you will not become complacent as the unholy system we have built returns as our focus.

George Barna has stated that spiritual revival in America has been stifled by at least five factors:

1. Spiritual complacency among believers,

2. Lifestyle comfort of non-believers,

3. Rejection of absolute moral truth,

4. No apparent difference between believers and non-believers, and;

5. No national and local cooperative effort among believers.

Those of us in men's ministry have been crying out

"like a voice in the wilderness" to be holy, obedient, and focused on God. Many men have turned to God in an unprecedented way, but what about the follow-up?

Following the terrorist attacks, people were "suddenly aware" of God; or their "lack of God." God wants us to lift the cross of Christ and work together to reach men in our cities. We are raising an army that is attacking the fortified walls of sin – sin in men that has darkened our families, cities, and nation.

Shortly after 9-11, I came to grips with the fact that this was not a movie. It's real life and it is the beginning of dangerous and perilous times that the Bible spoke about. It is a war without borders that will be fought by men, women, and children. This will not be a safe war where we send out the troops and read about it or see it on CNN from a comfortable distance, but one where we must engage in the battle in our everyday lives at work, in our travels, and in our own neighborhoods.

With my extensive background in the Secret Service, I understand all too well the threats and weaknesses of our open society. As we heard the first-hand reports of the firemen running up the stairs at the World Trade Center only to lose their lives in an attempt to save others, I felt the urgency to prepare a society for "a Holy War." Rescue workers' acts of bravery were that of unselfishness and should be the heart and spirit of Christians in America and around the world.

With prophetic reports of what may come, many of us feel the softness of our position in Christ and how we have allowed ourselves to get out of shape, spiritually. Many of us are a mere skeleton of dry bones. We need new life breathed into us by the Holy Spirit. We have become soft and comfortable in our Christian positions and we soon will feel the pain of conditioning ourselves for this new kind of war.

A holy war – one fought with zealots who are willing to die for their beliefs no matter the consequences. Fanatics who feel they are serving their god by their suicidal war, but I disagree. People generally will not purposefully die for a religion. They will die for a cause.

• Muslim fanatics fight a holy war and declare a "jihad" to defend their faith from what they perceive as the infidel spoiling their belief system.

• Jewish people of Israel fight a holy war because they know they are fighting for their own existence.

• Christians in America are not ready to fight a holy war. We have become too content and comfortable. We are not prepared for the cost.

How about you? Are you a true champion; or not? To successfully fight a holy war, we must be revived as a Christian nation. We say we are "One Nation Under God," but we don't act like a nation under God. We say, "In God We Trust," but it is just a motto. We truly do not believe it. If we believed it, we would live it. America has quit living as a godly nation. Our focus has shifted from God to ourselves.

Our families have disintegrated and our morals are compromised. We are an unholy nation and it is in the dollar that we trust. If there is any sense to be made from the tragedy of 9-11, it is that Americans are once again turning to God, but are we really? We must train ourselves to live according to the Word of God.

We are praying for our nation, and all who are impacted by the tragedy of 9-11 and the floods along the Gulf Coast. May we reach into the heart of God and know the peace of His freedom and love. We are calling for men to unite under the banner of God and the Lord Jesus to battle the enemy within and around our lives. We must retake our families for Christ and our nation for God. We must be committed to equip ourselves for a holy war.

Don't be content with the status quo. Be ready to ATTACK…the walls of sin, wherever they may be.

1. Are you too comfortable to be used by God?
2. Do you understand the concept that "the battle is the Lords."?
3. Are you complacent in your spiritual walk?
4. Can people recognize you as a true Believer or not?
5. Are you prepared to give your life for a genuine cause?
6. How do you shift your focus from self to God?

CHAPTER 14

ACCOUNTABILITY...
A Vital Need

Accountability was a "cornerstone" of the men's movement in the 1990's. There still is a tremendous need for us to be accountable, especially to God and our neighbors.

There is a need for sexual purity, an area that affects every man. Men are visual and enjoy beautiful things. Advertising agencies have long recognized this fact and use sex to appeal to our senses. Even the covers of regular publications use near-naked bodies to get our attention. The Swimsuit Edition of SPORTS ILLUSTRATED is their best-selling issue. Left alone, we will be drawn into a situation that is not pleasing to God. A lot of the times these situations are sexual encounters, either real or fantasy.

God's Word deals with this subject very specifically and thoroughly. We need the Word for instruction, but we also need the relationship of a friend to help us survive – someone to hold us accountable and sharpen our edge.

I encourage these relationships. Every man should be in a "Circle of Champions," close friends seeking God and keeping their focus sharp. Together, we can overcome the enemy. Jesus sent His disciples out in two's. This method helped them individually as much as it helped those to whom they ministered. There was accountability between them and they were an encouragement to one another.

Psalms 144:1 says, "Praise be the Lord my Rock, who

trains my hands for war, my fingers for battle." (NIV) We must examine what we put into our hands, and what our fingers are manipulating. The Word also says that a man should have clean hands and a pure heart.

With the increased use of computers and the Internet at our fingertips, the information age brings everything to our homes, and easily within our grasp. This sense of privacy allows us to go places on the Web where we would never go in person. We can hide in the obscurity of anonymity. Men should build in a system of accountability to temper their computer life.

We want to help men equip one another for real-life battles. We want to provide and plan battle plans that will help defeat the enemy and keep him away from your door. You need to have your hands trained for war and your fingers for battle. You need to develop relationships of accountability to help you make it through this life into eternal life.

No one can go it alone! Throughout my time in the United States Secret Service I was not only asked, but required to maintain accountability and work as a team with other agents. In working as teams we found ourselves to be better prepared and more equipped to fulfill the duties of our position. The saying that you are only as strong as your weakest link, is unfortunately all to real and quite accurate.

In the Secret Service we relied on our relationship with one another to fulfill the mission we were given and to grow as an individual. It was only through the team and accountability approach that we could faithfully protect the President and other leaders.

Accountability relationships are crucial to our success as Christian men. When Jesus sent out ministers and disciples, they went in groups of two. He wanted accountability and "iron sharpening iron."

When I entered the ministry, I quickly entered into relationships with other leaders, other pastors, and other men with a goal of surrounding myself with accountability. I needed them to push me to the next level and keep me from stumbling or loosing focus.

The most significant aspect of accountability relationships is inspiring your friend to take that next step daily to grow closer to God and to his family. We all need and want inspiration and encouragement. We all need someone to stand with us as we defend and stand firm for our families, our church, our pastor, and for our Lord.

Won't you be part of a relationship that is dedicated to help you fight your battles? Take that prayerful step of accountability, a positive step toward getting a grip on living a pure life.

Be a Champion and be part of a team, the Army of God.

1. To whom are you accountable?
2. How do you keep your focus sharp?
3. How do you guard yourself from the Enemy?

CHAPTER 15

SUCCESS...is a Team Effort

Success is the number one thing we as men use to judge ourselves. We feel a need to be successful in order to be significant to our families, our workplace, and the world. We rarely measure our success to be significant for God.

In his book, *Halftime*, Bob Buford says that men spend the first half of life trying to be successful and the last half searching for significance. As young men in the workplace, we are aggressive to "make our bones" and be recognized as a contributor to the success of the company or business and get promoted. It is, after all, the way men measure themselves.

This recognition helps us measure how successful we are. Another way we measure ourselves is the income we produce. We feel we must continually increase our income to keep up with inflation and the rising costs of providing for a family. Most men feel this is their number one priority as a husband and a father.

Although being the provider is obviously very important, so is your responsibility to a lifestyle of consecration to an almighty and sovereign God.

Men look at life as a set of goals. Once we reach one, we set off to achieve another. If we fall short of a goal, we have failed and depression can set into our lives. We don't recognize that success is not a destination – it is a lifetime journey.

The measure of a man in God's eyes is entirely different than how we measure ourselves. He sees us as friend, partner, and son. He wants to be in relationship with us, guide us and help us when we look for an answer. Success in God's eyes is calling on Him, depending on Him, and seeking Him first in all things. He tells us that we are running a race that is marked out for us. He doesn't want us to take short cuts. He wants us to follow His route.

In the way we are wired as men, we want to try everything in our own strength first. If that doesn't work, then we call on God to fix it or ask Him to bless our plans. We want to be significant, but we measure it in a secular way. It is only after our total surrender to God that we start getting breakthroughs in the confusion we call life. Significance starts meaning different things as we begin to measure our lives with the Word of God.

Being successful in God's eyes is our number one focus… in God's eyes! We want to help men connect with God, strengthen them in God's Word, and move them into godly relationships with other men and with God Himself.

We want to build male leaders in the church, men in leadership who will take up the call to work alongside their pastors and others to reach the world for Christ. We measure our success of a man by the desire in his heart to be closer to God tomorrow than he is today. This is a man who runs the race God has laid out for him. Are you such a man? Are you successful in God's eyes?

1. What is your ultimate goal in life?
2. What are the daily goals that you would like to change?
3. How do you measure success?
4. How do you "measure up" another man?
5. Are you spiritually successful, in God's eyes?
6. Are you destined to be a true champion?

CHAPTER 16

REFLECTIONS...
of the Men's Movement

I can remember early in my walk as a man of God watching videos of Ed Cole talking about being a man of God in everything we do as men. I remember when Coach McCartney first called for men to come to a stadium and repent. I can remember when my awareness of the magnitude of the Men's Movement so overwhelmed me that my heart opened up to serve God full time with all my heart.

These times of memory enrich me as a man because they are special times when God touched my heart as a man. The "grandfather" of the Men's Movement, Dr. Edwin Louis Cole, was so generous of his time and never was too busy to stop and talk about what God was doing in my life. I asked him early on in my ministry when the men's movement first started to mentor me in how to follow God. We would talk by phone or share a meal and discuss the successes and failures of ministering to men. He shared how his vision of men's ministry had come to life with HonorBound and things that he wanted to see 20 years ago were finally happening.

The purpose of men's ministries is to raise up dead men, shake their dry bones, put "skin" on their skeleton through training, and breathe new life through the power of the Holy Spirit.

I also remember when I was still with the Secret Service in Seattle, Washington and Coach Bill McCartney came to the Northwest to speak to a gathering of pastors. I was asked to be his escort and provide him security. I had met him other times when involved in other Promise Keepers' conferences but this one was special. I had just been called by God to step out of the Secret Service and serve Him full time. Coach found out about my "waiting on God" and prayed with me about God's plan for me in the men's movement. He concluded very quietly saying: "It is going to be very good working with you. You are passionate about this as I am." A few weeks later I was asked to lead an international men's movement.

I feel honored to be in a league with these men and ministries; and even more honored to serve an awesome God. He wants us to follow him and lead men and their families to Him. Won't you join me as we walk in a lifestyle of champions!

1. How has the recent men's movement affected your life?
2. What are you doing to continue that men's movement through YOU?

CHAPTER 17

CHAMPIONS OF HONOR...
Men in Revival: Complacent Christians or Prayer Warriors?

In today's church, young men grow up in youth groups and when they grow away from the youth ranks, many fall away from the church and God. They don't see a place for them in the church that compares to the fun and excitement of the youth group. The youth group's spiritual bonding fades as members go different ways in life.

When a young man looks to the church, he doesn't see where he belongs. If you ask him to get involved in the men's groups, he'll respond, "No thanks, that's the old man's club!" There is no identity for him in the church. He starts to feel the need to experience life, but this is when he really needs God and the church in his life. Some of life's most important choices and decisions are made during this period and it is not the time for young men to feel distant from God and Christian friends. In college or on the job they have more and more encounters with the world. Now is the time to be in revival and a time to draw near to God. He wants to raise young champions, re-fired by the Spirit of God.

Today, men desire a spiritual revival led by men. For this to happen, the expectations of men must change. We can't continue to delegate responsibility for the spiritual well being of our families just to the pastor or our wives while we earn a living or satisfy personal goals. We must recognize our responsibility, step up to the plate, and strengthen our relationship with God. We can't hide as Adam did in the Garden. God wants us to be champions.

The young man is no exception. There is no grace period during which a young man can go out and experience the world to "sow those wild oats." That is a lie from the devil. We have become self-centered, lacking faith and compassion, disobedient, and unfaithful to God. Men need to be in revival and we need it now. We need to see the manliness of serving God with more passion and fervor than cheering on our favorite team.

Charles Finney describes revival in his book, *Finney on Revival*, as "nothing else than a new beginning of obedience to God." Finney also says that "a revival may be expected when Christians have a spirit of prayer for revival and may be expected whenever Christians are found willing to make the *sacrifices* necessary to carry it on. It consists of two parts: as it respects the church and as it respects the ungodly."

Noah Webster, in his *American Dictionary of the English Language* (c.1828), defines revival as "an awakening of men to their spiritual concerns." He also describes revival as "return or recall to activity from a state of languor." Many of us in the American church are in need of revival. We are in a "state of languor!" A better word for it could be complacency.

Complacency lulls us into a false sense of spiritual security. We become content with the position we occupy or the depth of our spiritual lives. Moses was complacent while tending sheep on the backside of the mountain. When God asked him to return to Egypt to free His people, Moses argued with God about his qualifications.

One might say that Moses was content or complacent in his life, satisfied with his role as husband and shepherd. God came to him in a burning bush to call him out. We need a burning bush to call us out to free God's people from the lure of Satan.

The **Complacent Christian** is one of the biggest problems in the church today. Complacent Christians often live off the "fat" of the land—a yesterday experience with God that impacted us and drew us to Him. Something we haven't experienced again in a while, but we keep looking for it to reappear and draw us once again close to God. We keep looking back for God but He is not behind us. He is right there, in front of us. We are living in our past experiences when what we really need is revival! We can't have revival if we keep comparing it to past experiences. The encounter with God is within us and not an "event." Don't rest on what you had. Rather look forward to what is to come. Be strengthened in the power of the Spirit that is within you.

Our talk about revival is directed toward the Christian – a move of God in our lives that makes us feel the presence of God as we have before. We long to recapture that feeling of being close to God and walking in His shadow. We seek to revisit that time at the altar, remembering when our prayers were answered in a powerful way. Many of us live in these past times and become "complacent Christians".

Webster's dictionary defines complacent as "to be satisfied." I never want to be just satisfied with God in my life. I want more of Him, to be near Him, grow in Him, always expectant of His soon coming return. I don't want to be satisfied with what He has done in my life, but look with expectant eyes for Him to guide my every move. If we keep looking back we'll have a stale sense of God's presence in our lives and we risk becoming "lukewarm and spit out," as the Bible describes.

Overcoming complacency requires discipline. We must train ourselves to be subject to God and not to the flesh. It is a daily process. Physically, without exercise and a proper diet, you become fat. The same is true spiritually; you must exercise daily with a steady disciplined diet, in order to conquer "Spiritual Flesh Fat." Without training, spiritual fat will re-appear. Training requires daily sacrifice.

The Bible says *"Therefore I urge you, brothers, in view of God's mercy, to offer your bodies as living sacrifices, holy and pleasing to God – this is your spiritual act of worship."* (Romans 12:1 NIV)

The footnotes for this passage in the *Full Life Study Bible*, state, "Believers must possess a single-minded passion to please God in love, devotion, praise and holiness, and to offer their bodies for His service. Our greatest desire should be to live lives of holiness and to be accepted by God. We must live for God, worship him, obey him, take his side against sin and for righteousness, resist and hate evil, perform works of kindness for others, imitate Christ, follow him, serve him, live by the Spirit, and be filled with the Spirit. We must offer our bodies to God as dead to sin and as the temple of the Holy Spirit."

The Secret Service taught me to react contrary to human nature; to put myself in between the person I was protecting and danger. Literally "standing in the line of fire." Being able to become a shield when bullets are fired does not happen overnight. It takes discipline and training.

The normal reaction is to "get small" and take cover, not "get large" and protect. Reacting to protect requires dedication to duty, consistent practice of reactions to real-life situations, conditioning yourself not to think before reacting, and reacting according to your training. Training is the difference between life and death. Not yours, but the person you are sworn to protect.

As champions, applying this principle through the Word and Holy Spirit allows us to react to real-life situations according to the way God desires; training ourselves to react according to His teaching. The daily sacrifices of spending time in the Word, prayer, worship, and fellowship are needed to prevent the "Spiritual Flesh Fat" of the world from re-appearing in our lives. This discipline and training brings revival to our lives. We will not and cannot be complacent when we submit to this discipline. This discipline develops "expectant living."

Men need to feel *Expectant in Christ* or be an **Expectant Christian**. This kind of living has us searching for God's fresh "manna" of the day, devouring the Word as a fresh meal, and seeking nourishment from God in a life-changing way. *Expectant Christians* continue to go after God for more of His presence, become obedient to His Word, and live daily in the power of the Holy Spirit. An expectant Christian is a genuine champion. They realize there are spiritual battles in their lives, but depend on the Holy Spirit to give them power to overcome. They recognize the battle comes from the enemy. Training in God's Word pays off here. It allows the believer to react to Satan's attacks according to the Word and directed by the Holy Spirit.

As we press closer to God, we start to become a **Transparent Christian**. Transparent Christians are *trained prayer warriors* who walk with God in such a way that people see God in everything they do. Their lives are so transparent their problems are not seen, but God's majesty and might are seen in everything they do. Transparent Christians are recognized by the devil as fervent and effective prayer warriors; men striving to hear with God's ears, see with God's eyes, and feel with God's heart. Everything has eternal value. We cannot do this alone. We need iron to sharpen iron, other people to interact and minister with and keep us accountable. We strive to be holy because He is holy. We become Champions of Honor, refined by the fire of the Lord by being in His presence, prayer warriors ready for battle.

Prayer warriors have to:

1. Be clear minded and self controlled, so they can pray (1 Peter 4:7 NIV)

2. Live godly lives (2Peter 3:10,14,17 NIV)

3. Become *living sacrifices* (Romans 12:1 NIV)

4. Pray in the Holy Spirit (Jude18-23 NIV)

5. Become *holy because He is holy* (1Peter 1:13-16 NIV).

We don't need to "do" church; we need to BE the church. We need to die to ourselves and live for Jesus. We need to be "DEAD MEN RISING!"

In a world where there is constant focus on pleasing the consumer, we must be consumed by His presence and therefore pleasing God. If the "things" and "events" of this world consume us, we will eventually be consumed by the world. If God and His Word consume us, we will never be consumed by the world, but have everlasting life with Jesus Christ. We need others to surround us and keep us impregnable.

Secret Service agents work formations around those they protect. These formations are designed to have overlapping coverage so that if one falls or is taken out by the enemy, others can still accomplish the mission. Agents work as a team watching other's areas as well their own so that no weak areas exist. Imagine concentric circles surrounding the center. The center has the most protection, gradually moving outward toward lesser protection. The center is always pure. Nothing contaminates the "safe zone".

If the Holy Spirit dwells within us, then we need to keep our center (heart) pure from the world. In that circle is the Holy Spirit who gives us power but will not dwell with sin.

In the next circle out would be our discipline in the Word, training with our prayer partners, our family, or accountability partners that help keep us safe and overcome temptation.

Then finally beyond that circle are those that we minister to, people or ministries that strengthen us because of our relationship with them. It takes teamwork as Christians, men depending on each other to help them guard their hearts. The devil is out to rob, steal, and destroy, and we need to intensify our efforts to work together against his plans.

Remember our Father has *"plans to prosper you and not to harm you, plans to give you hope and a future. Then you will call upon me and come and pray to me, and I will listen to you. You will seek me and find me when you seek me with all your heart. I will be found by you," declares the Lord, "and will bring you back from captivity."* (Jeremiah 29:11-14a NIV)

All men, but especially young men, need to intensify efforts to live apart from the trappings of the world. Don't walk away from God or the church because you don't feel you fit in, but set the example as a Champion of God, a "Prayer Warrior", ready to battle the world's influence in our lives. Be a warrior going into the workplace for God, living a pure and holy life, innocent of the evil that surrounds you, and a warrior that is the light in a lost and dying world. If you shine as a prayer warrior by being transparent, then God will shine through you as a champion. This will help bring revival to our churches and our world.

Vince Lombardi said, "The quality of a person's life is in direct proportion to their commitment to excellence, regardless of their chosen field of endeavor." The quality that God gives us is eternal and does not fade away. Men, it is time to commit to the battle ahead, preparing for God's army, and readying for the soon coming return of our Commander-in-Chief.

The Apostle Paul said it best, *"And do this, understanding the present time. The hour has come for you to wake up from your slumber, because our salvation is nearer now than when we first believed. The night is nearly over; the day is almost here. So let us put aside the deeds of darkness and put on the armor of light. Let us behave decently, as in the daytime, not in orgies and drunkenness, not in sexual immorality and debauchery, not in dissension and jealousy. Rather, clothe yourselves with the Lord Jesus Christ, and do not think about how to gratify the desires of the sinful nature." (Romans 13:11-14 NIV)*

Men – all men, young and old – are being called to holiness, set apart from this world, obedient to God's Word, and living in such a way that precipitates a revival such as we have never seen before. Our society cannot stand for things to remain the same. They must change. According to current studies, 40% of our homes are fatherless, an unacceptable statistic in a country where our slogan is "one nation under God." Are we really that? Other nations that do not proclaim Jesus as Lord have more family values than we do. Our country is like Israel when it wandered in the desert, the miracles of God all around them but still going after other gods and idols.

Men! – The greatest mission field, during these times, is MEN!

<u>Why have men chosen to live in the world by the world's standards?</u> Because men are filled with disappointments, a lack of Christian leadership in their homes, demonic and worldly pressures to succeed, constantly changing values and priorities, no discipline, and most men have no penetrating Christian relationships.

<u>How do we reach men in a secular world?</u> The answers are prayer and example! If our prayers are to be effective then we must remove sin from our lives. If the sin is out, then the example will be apparent. Striving to live a holy life is an example to men living in the world and it attracts them to God.

<u>Why is integrity important in men?</u> We have to be a living example. Even when we fail, it is important that we get up and continue with God. We have to recognize the failure, ask God for forgiveness, and continue to serve God. Other men will see this and realize they too can walk with a forgiving and loving God. They will see

you as human and approachable. They don't have to run away from God, but to Him as a Father. The problem is that many men do not have a good image of their earthly father. This has to change and our example of godly ways can help effect this needed change.

<u>Why is it important to minister to men?</u> Most men feel the need for ministry, but are unable to express it in a "manly" way. The breakdown of the family is largely due to the lack of a godly example in the home and the lack of God in the home to bind it together. Men want to be needed but have trouble expressing need. We are taught to be self- sufficient.

Remember, with a man comes his family! When men begin to operate in the full strength of God, his family, community, workplace, and nation benefit. Also, as the man becomes the spiritual leader of the home, Satan's attacks on him and that home will come more frequently and more intensely. He will need other men to surround him with prayer support.

Men must be focused on God and not the world or our selfish desires. Young men face an uphill climb without godly examples, a complacent church, and the impact of a "Fatherless Society."

It is up to you, a resurrected champion in the Army of God, to make a difference in our society.

1. What was your "burning bush" experience that awakened you to your purpose for life?
2. Are you considered a "complacent Christian" or a "Prayer Warrior?"
3. How do you specifically minister to other men?

ABOUT THE AUTHOR

Charles A. (Chuck) Brewster founded Champions of Honor in January 2005, a ministry focused upon men and their relationship with God. Chuck is presently serving as the Men's Pastor at Brownsville Church, in Pensacola, FL and a missionary to men-worldwide. He speaks at various functions and conferences nationally and internationally.

Prior to moving to Pensacola, Chuck had been the National Director of HonorBound: Men of Promise for seven years. During that time he built a sustained foundation for ministry to men for the Assemblies of God. Recognized as the Men's Ministry of the Year by the National Coalition of Men's Ministry, and Chuck was honored in 2004 with a lifetime achievement award from the Mighty Men of Valor, a multicultural organization of pastors and men.

Chuck was born and raised in Pensacola, Florida. He served with the Pensacola, Florida and Birmingham, Alabama police departments. Chuck is a graduate of Florida State University with a degree in Social Welfare and Criminology, and also a graduate of the 'Contemporary Executive Development Program' at George Washington University, School of Business and Public Management.

MASTERPLAN
for God's Champions

Today in America over 38% of our children go to bed at night without a father in the home. As the recent Presidential elections showed, Americans are concerned about the downward spiral of our moral values. The majority of men are not the spiritual leaders in their homes. We must do something about this condition.

We can reach every family in America, one man at a time. Statistics have shown that if we reach a man for Christ over 90% of the time he will reach his entire family for Christ. If this statistic is true we can grow men, who grow their families, who grow their churches, who grow the Kingdom of God.

"Champions of Honor" brings a focused ministry to men who desire to develop their Biblical masculinity into a stronger relationship with God and other men. It is grounded in Biblical and men's relational resources that will train and prepare men toward being commissioned as "Ministers to Men." Every man has a champion within him. Discovering and developing that champion is the challenge.

VISION

Reaching every family, one man at a time!

Our research has found only 1 in every 18 men in America are in a mentoring process. The studies have shown that when a man is reached for Christ, he will lead his entire family to Christ over 90% of the time. Our goal is to mentor and develop men by challenging their masculine spirit. In order to do that, we must help them discover and develop their Biblical masculinity. If we just gave them a 'macho' boost to their already elevated worldly ego, then we will have failed them. "By building a network of men who minister to men, we accomplish far more than we ever could alone. The exponential growth potential of a network of this kind can do much to further the kingdom of God, reach families and turn the pendulum of America back to biblical values and discipleship. Too many children go to bed at night, absent their biological father; too many moral failures of leaders and men are occurring; too many marriages are ending in divorce; loneliness and depression are becoming an epidemic spread throughout men. It is time to change this trend. By committing ourselves to God and becoming equipped to be used by God, we can reach men through discipleship and bring men, families and America back to God."

MISSION

The three-fold objective of Champions of Honor is to help men:
- Discover and Develop Biblical Manhood and Values.
- Discover and Develop the Champion within us.
- Discover and Reveal the Father to the Fatherless

Every man that aligns with Champions of Honor must "pay the price of championship" as Ed Cole said in his book, Courage. He must commit to grow in Christ through God's Word and "masculine context" resources that develop an honorable man into a Champion. It is time for men to quit being spiritual wimps and develop as warriors for Christ. Each man must be a man of vision, understand the meaning of unity on the team, be disciplined and faithful, be an inspiration to others, and persevere with character to the finish.

Each man must do the following to be a commissioned Champion of Honor:

• Acquire pastoral approval and sign a covenant with his pastor to be a Champion. (Downloadable on website)

• Complete 12 units of the recommended "Champions of Honor" resources. (Located on website)

• Be involved in a Champions Circle, Letting Iron Sharpen Iron.

• Becoming a Champion of Missions, supporting worthy missions outreaches or organizations.

COMMISSIONING SERVICE

After completing the development cycle and fulfilling all the above requirements, *Champions of Honor* ministry and the local church will schedule a commissioning service where the Champion will be honored and presented a Champions Sword symbolic of a warrior with the Word. A commissioning service is a time to honor the men who have shown their commitment to grow as godly men and, in return, desire to minister to men.

The Champion is presented with a Champions of Honor- Sword during a ceremony honoring his faithfulness and perseverance. The commissioning service can be done within the local church, during a men's event or at a national conference. As a Commissioned Man, you will then be expected to reach three other men and mentor them through the Champions of Honor challenge, thus growing the body of Christ, one man at a time.

CHARTERS

Churches that Charter with Champions of Honor and register their men into Champions, will become a member of the Champions of Honor Network. COH will provide leadership training, vision casting, coaching, mentoring and help each network church link into the Champions of Honor website with information about their chapter specific for their church. Network Churches and Champions will also be invited to special gatherings of Champions or can schedule a Champions of Honor Weekend or Conference.

Please consider allowing Champions of Honor to work with you and your leadership in this endeavor. Champions of Honor, Inc. is a Florida Not-for-Profit Charitable Ministry.

If this book has adjusted your thinking
or impacted your daily life,
or you would like to comment,
please contact us:

CHAMPIONS OF HONOR
P. O. Box 820
Gulf Breeze, FL 32562

For more information about Champions,
please visit our website at:
www.championsofhonor.com